BEGINNING GOD

J-O-T-T-I-N-G-S
from
GENESIS

William Hartley

BAKER BOOK HOUSE
Grand Rapids, Michigan

ISBN: 0-8010-4132-5
Copyright 1975 by Baker Book House Company

THIS BOOK IS DEDICATED TO ALL
MISSIONARIES WORLDWIDE WHO HAVE GIVEN THEIR
LIVES FOR THE TELLING OF THE GOOD NEWS THAT
JESUS CHRIST, THE SON OF GOD, GAVE HIS LIFE
THAT MEN AND WOMEN MAY KNOW THE TRUTH OF
GOD.

ALL THE AUTHOR'S PROFITS FROM THIS BOOK SHALL
GO TO THOSE MISSIONARIES SO DESIGNATED BY THE
AUTHOR OR HIS WIFE.

*And moreover, because the preacher was wise, he still taught
the people knowledge; yea, he gave good heed, and sought
out, and set in order many proverbs. The preacher sought to
find out acceptable words: and that which was written was
upright, even words of truth (Eccles. 12:9-10).*

CONTENTS

Foreword

Preface

Acknowledgments

1. In the Beginning 9
2. That's How It Was 11
3. Hath God Said? 13
4. A Man from the Lord 16
5. The Record Is Kept 18
6. It Came to Pass 20
7. All Things Ready 22
8. Not Forgotten 24
9. Bountiful Blessings 26
10. Continuing Records 28
11. One Speech 30
12. Evading the Call 32
13. Up and Out 36
14. It Happened Again 37
15. Nothing Stops 38
16. Barrenness or Births 41
17. No Limits with God 43
18. The Unexpected 45
19. Divine Intervention 47
20. Going On Toward? 49
21. Fulfillment 51
22. Still More to Come 52
23. The Faithful God 54
24. Fullness in All Things 56
25. Divine Renewal 58

26. Like Father—Like Son 60
27. Parental Responsibility 63
28. Separation 65
29. We Must Go On 67
30. Fruitfulness or Else 69
31. Transferred Glory 71
32. Going Forward to Meet God 73
33. Looking—Fear or Faith? 75
34. Big Doors Turn on Little Hinges 77
35. No Sitting Down 79
36. The Origin of Evil 81
37. Dwelling in the Land 83
38. Running Away 85
39. The Fulfillment of Dreams 87
40. Where Are My Visions? 89
41. Time Will Tell 91
42. You Do Something About It 93
43. Adversity a Blessing 95
44. Empty Stomachs—Full Sacks 97
45. The Love of Jesus 99
46. The Last Pilgrimage 101
47. Identification—My Father 103
48. The Hands of Benediction 105
49. Sons of God Have a Future 107
50. Ultimate Devotion—Worship 109

FOREWORD

Genesis is the seedbed of the Bible. Every great move of history, every important doctrine and aspect of God's dealings with men can be traced back to this epic document. It is the book of origins—of original nature and original sin; of the origin of nations and the beginning of divine dispensations. Jesus referred to Genesis in His teaching on marriage and divorce; Paul found in Genesis the roots of his great doctrine of justification by faith. Genesis is a source book.

And what an army of patriarchs and pilgrims march through its pages! Genesis is a living gallery of biography—terse, tense and meaningful life stories that demonstrate God's methods with men, and man's response to God. It shows that faith is more than fame, and true greatness lies in spiritual maturity.

Genesis, too, is a wonderful book of devotion. The author of this volume, in commenting on the first verse of each chapter of this remarkable book, draws out and applies the latent lessons. Reading Genesis again with this helpful book to prompt us will make the ancient Scriptures more real and significant to us in these modern times.

Aaron Linford
Editor, *Redemption Tidings*

PREFACE

These writings were not, in the first place, intended for publication. Originally they were for my own personal devotion as I read the Word of God each morning. As I read, I wrote, and that inspirationally. So the manuscript grew and finally I submitted it to Aaron Linford, editor of *Redemption Tidings,* who accepted it for a weekly devotional page. There was no attempt at literary quality, nor was it my idea to write a theological sermon; they were purely for inspirational purposes, and that is why some are shorter than others. I received many letters from those who found a measure of blessing in these jottings. Many, also many friends in other lands, requested that they be put into book form as a more permanent source of blessing. So here is the book.

I pray that you will find in this book that which will bless your soul and meet your needs spiritually each time you read it (You will find, I am sure, that it is a "re-readable" book.) and that you will be as blessed in the reading of this little volume as I have been in the writing of it. God bless you.

William Hartley

ACKNOWLEDGMENTS

My deep appreciation is expressed to my ministerial friend, advisor, encourager, and helper, Aaron Linford, editor of *Redemption Tidings,* who has been a constant source of encouragement to me by publishing so much of what I submitted to him. My wife also has encouraged me to put these writings in its present form.

I cannot express in words my gratitude to Eleanor Slevkoff, of South-Gate, California, who freely gave of her time to type and edit the manuscript. Also to Fred Carter of Pomona, California, who was responsible for the magnificent artwork on the cover. Then, not as though it was the last thought, but because without Him there could have been no work at all, I am thankful to God who inspired these people to help produce this book. God bless you all.

1. IN THE BEGINNING

Genesis Chapter One, Verse One.
"In the beginning God created the heaven
and the earth."

"In the beginning God." When men want an
answer to the universe and all the mysteries related
to it, unless they start here in their investigations,
they are soon lost in a maze of confusing theories.

Without God, everything becomes just a theory,
a probability, a "maybe." When we start with God,
we have the answer to most of the problems of the
universe in which we live. When men make a dis-
covery, they discover that which has been from the
beginning. There was no evolving of the laws of the
universe, God made them at the beginning, and
what they were then, they still remain today. The
sun, the moon, and the stars all fulfill the design
that was planned by God in the beginning. The
natural laws do not go into reverse. The sun always
rises in the east and always sets in the west. Man
cannot change the order of these laws. There are
clouds, and only from the clouds does rain fall upon
the earth. You could go on with numerous un-
changing laws of creation, and each time you
would always trace them back to God in the beginning. Men have used these laws—harnessed them
by their own ingenuity, and all of mankind has
benefited as a result. Should God at any time
change the laws of creation, society as it is today

would crumble and collapse. Man would have to start all over again to discover the new laws.

So all life begins with God. Before man was, God was. We can point to a time when man began. We can discover from the rocks and from the earth that man had a beginning. Yet in the beginning, God. He was before all things. So we begin with God. We continue with God. And so in the end of time, and throughout eternity, it will still be—*God*.

2. THAT'S HOW IT WAS

Genesis Chapter Two, Verse One.
"Thus the heavens and the earth were
finished, and all the host of them."

"Thus"—that is how it was. That is how it is
—and who is that man who would dare to contend
with the Creator of the universe? This fact cannot
be contended about; it is without argument. Thus
God did it, and not only did it, but He finished it.
Whatever the Lord God begins, He always
finishes. It was God who planned our salvation,
even before the foundation of the world. The time
element with God is no problem at all. God set the
seasons and the years for our benefit. He gave us
the night before He gave us the day. Oh, the wisdom of God! The time of rest before the time of
work. He made for us a day of rest, one day every
seven days, a Sabbath made for man, to rest his
body, to rest his mind, and to refresh his spirit in
communion and fellowship with his Creator.
When a man violates his days of rest, he violates his
mind and his body, and he leaves God out of his
life.

Thus the heavens were finished. God finished
them for us. Then on the cross of Calvary, Jesus
took our sins and paid the total price for our redemption. Jesus cried with a loud voice, "It is
finished." It is finished for us—for you, for me.

'Tis finished—all the debt is paid,
  Justice divine is satisfied.
The grand and full atonement made,
  Christ for a guilty world has died.

3. HATH GOD SAID?

> *Genesis Chapter Three, Verse One.*
> "Now the serpent was more subtil than any beast of the field which the Lord God had made. And he said unto the woman, Yea, hath God said, Ye shall not eat of every tree of the garden?"

The subtilty of the devil is endless. He has practiced the art of deception for so long that God calls him "that deceiver" (Rev. 12:9; 13:14; 20:10). "Hath God said?" With this the devil constantly challenges you to doubt the Word of God. He came in exactly the same way to Jesus: *"If* thou be the Son of God . . . " (Matt. 4:6). Jesus had no need to prove to the devil who He was. Jesus knew who He was. The devil knew who He was, too. Self-vindication is to prove what we are. This does not make us any more than we already are. Every believer is just what the Word of God says he is. We have what it says we have. We can do what God says we can do. To do what the Lord says we must not do will only bring us loss. We are not called to prove anything that God says we are. In fact, we would prove nothing at all except that we are doubters of His Word. Doubting the Word of God is the worst kind of poison that one can take into his system. God has said it, and that is it. It is enough that we believe it.

Let us "be sober, be vigilant; because your adversary the devil, as a roaring lion, walketh about, seeking whom he may devour" (1 Peter 5:8). The

13

devil is *subtil*, a *deceiver*, a *liar*, an *adversary*. We must ever be on the alert. The purpose of Satan is to get us away from the simplicity that is in Christ. "But I fear, lest by any means, as the serpent beguiled Eve through his subtilty, so your minds should be corrupted from the simplicity that is in Christ" (2 Cor. 11:3). The devil will go to any length to bring about the downfall of God's people. He will even go to the extent impersonating that which is good: "And no marvel; for Satan himself is transformed into an angel of light" (2 Cor. 11:14). The Word of God is our safety and guidance in all things.

The strategy of the devil is generally to attack when we are alone. This is one of the many good reasons why we should keep in fellowship with those of like mind, the people of God. "Two are better than one . . . for if they fall, the one will lift up his fellow: but woe to him that is alone when he falleth; for he hath not another to help him up" (Eccles. 4:9-10). It was through that very same channel, through the woman being alone, that the devil spoiled Adam. The devil was later to be spoiled by the seed of the woman. "But when the fulness of time was come, God sent forth his Son, made of a woman" (Gal. 4:4). This was the beginning of the end for Satan, our adversary. "In that day the Lord with his sore and great and strong sword shall punish leviathan the piercing serpent, even leviathan that crooked serpent" (Isa. 27:1). "And I saw an angel come down from heaven, having the key of the bottomless pit and a great chain in his hand. And he laid hold on the dragon,

14

that old serpent, which is the Devil, and Satan, and bound him a thousand years" (Rev. 20:1-2).

So let us watch . . .

4. A MAN FROM THE LORD

Genesis Chapter Four, Verse One.
"And Adam knew Eve his wife; and she conceived, and bare Cain, and said, I have gotten a man from the Lord."

"I have gotten a man from the Lord." There seems to be in these words an expression from Eve of joy and gladness. She senses that God has pardoned, and in His pardon has blessed them with this son. It is the name they give to the boy that reflects the spirit of giving to God the glory. It is the evidence of their thankfulness for having been given this life to care for. Again it shows to us the evidence of rising up out of failure. God is being put first. How much we need to recognize this in our everyday life. Even when we have been guilty of failure, there is always the fact that He is waiting for us to tell Him we are sorry for our conduct, for our sin. We have His promise that He will forgive. "If we confess our sins, he is faithful and just to forgive us our sins, and to cleanse us from all unrighteousness" (1 John 1:9). When we fail, and analyze the reason, we will discover it was because we did not put God first.

So when you are conscious of failing the Lord, don't sit down in your failure, but come to Him. As we confess our failure, He will forgive and restore. Afterwards, let us show Him the evidence that we have learned our lesson.

To put God first is to save ourselves from trouble.
Let us put God first in all things, all the time.

5. THE RECORD IS KEPT

Genesis Chapter Five, Verse One.
"This is the book of the generations of Adam. In the day that God created man, in the likeness of God made he him."

God keeps His records straight and clear. Here is the record of the mainstream of man. There must have been others, but they were only auxiliary. All men were a part of His plan, but in this record, only the main ones are mentioned. These are from Adam to and until Noah's line. "In the day." This speaks of a period of time, rather than our twenty-four-hour day. We have all, from Adam until Noah, been included in the day, because of His word. "This is the book of the generations." That day begins with the one day that God created Adam, and made him in His likeness. "And God said, let us make man in our image, after our likeness . . . so God created man in his own image, in the image of God created he him" (Gen. 1:26-27). The word *image* is best described as "a visual counterpart; a representation." When we consider this for a moment, we are sure to be shaken from any complacency that we may have. Ask yourselves the question, "Am I a representation of God? Am I a visual counterpart of God?" Then we soon see why so few, in comparison to the many, really believe in the reality of God. God will become real to others as I become real in God and God is made real in me and through me. It is no wonder that Jesus said to Philip and to all His disciples, "If ye had known me, ye should have known my Father also . . . he that hath seen me hath seen the Father also . . . Believest thou not that I am in the Father, and the Father in me? Believe me that I am in the Father, and the Father in me" (John 14:7-11).

We lost the likeness that God had given to man; we lost the part of us that was a visual counterpart, the representation of God in us. That is why it is absolutely necessary for us to be born again. We need Christ. Without Christ, we are without hope and without God (Eph. 2:12). But in Christ, and with Christ in us "we are made nigh by the blood of Christ" (Eph. 2:13); "In whom ye also are builded together for an habitation of God through the Spirit" (Eph. 2:22).

6. IT CAME TO PASS

Genesis Chapter Six, Verse One.
"And it came to pass, when men began to multiply on the face of the earth, and daughters were born unto them."

There are many times in the Scripture where it says, "And it came to pass." Sometimes it is said in the sense of the fulfillment of some promise that God had made in the past. We can be well assured that if the Lord has declared it, then it will come to pass. Here it came to pass because of something that men brought in. Primarily it was the simple function of fulfilling the commission of the Lord, "Be fruitful and multiply, and replenish the earth, and subdue it: and have dominion." This command, given to man in his unfallen state, still remained in force when he became a fallen creature, having been restored by God through sacrifice to a fellowship with God on the grounds of that sacrifice. So, then, Adam produced only his own kind: "For as by one man's disobedience many were made sinners . . ." (Rom. 5:19). It is here we have the declaration "It came to pass, when men began to multiply." So the result was that we have a multiplication of sons of Adam, or a multiplication of sinners, and as the following verses reveal, there were many who refused the way of righteousness for the way of sin and wrongdoing. This ultimately brought about the full destruction of all but eight persons after something like a thousand years of warnings from God, and one hundred and twenty years of strong preaching by Noah. When man saw that he was strong by numerical values, it was then that he "felt" strong. He did not seem to understand that he was only as strong as he was within himself. He had forgotten that all he had and all he was or ever could be depended on the mercy of God.

We can see this not only in ourselves, but among our fellowships and our churches. When we were small we were more dependent on God. The stronger we grew, the prouder we got. Yes, prouder—but not prouder of God, but of *our* progress, *our* attainments, and *our* numerical strength. We forgot that we were only as strong as each individual member. King David failed on this very same point. "Let not the wise man glory in his wisdom, neither let the mighty man glory in his might, let not the rich man glory in his riches, but let him glory in this, that he understandeth and knoweth me, that I am the Lord which exercise lovingkindness in the earth; for in these things I delight, saith the Lord" (Jer. 9:22-23). It was said also to be the failing of King Uzziah. It is recorded of him, "He was marvelously helped til he was strong, but when he was strong, his heart was lifted up" (2 Chron. 26:15-16). Let us watch that it is not written of us in this manner, "And it came to pass, *when . . .*"

7. ALL THINGS READY

Genesis Chapter Seven, Verse One.
"And the Lord said unto Noah, Come thou and all thy house into the ark; for thee have I seen righteous before me in this generation."

After Noah had spent years believing the promise of God, preaching the word of God, and preparing the ark, the Lord spoke to him again. There had been silent years—years of unrecorded events. First there was given the word of the promised judgment, the promised protection in the covenant, but time had to elapse before these promises were fulfilled. We see that this occurs more than once in the Word of God. God gives voice to His promise, then there is the silent period. The silent weeks, the silent months, the silent years. Nothing seems to be happening. Has God forgotten? Have you ever experienced such a time? You have received the promise from the Lord and then it seemed that there was no sign at all of the fulfilling of the promise. You are not the only one. You wondered, but you still believed—and then came the answer. There was Elijah by the brook at the command of the Lord. Two and a half years slipped by. The only evidence he had that things were alright were that the ravens arrived each morning and each evening. Then the ravens no longer came, but the word of the Lord came again. It was moving day. When we have the promise of the Lord, whatever the promise might be, whether it be for deliverance or for judgment, He will surely speak again, and it will be moving day. It seems that it will not be long before it is moving day for the church. Jesus said He would come again. All around us are the evidences of His preparation. One day He will say, "It is moving day. All things are ready. Are you ready for *Me?*"

"Come thou and all thy house." The invitation is to all. It is God's perfect plan. It is His will that not one of our family should be left out of the great plan of salvation. Redemption was planned for all. The sacrifice was big enough for all. The price was paid that the debt of every sin of every sinner be atoned for. It was fully paid by the shedding of the blood of the Lord Jesus Christ. As in the days of Noah, so it is now, faith in the spoken word of God is the requirement. To believe God's word meant turning away from sin, repenting, confessing, and believing that God meant what He said. He is still saying, "Come thou and all thy house." The invitation was valid until the door was shut, then it was withdrawn. He still says, "Come!"—"Come unto me, all ye that labor" (Matt. 11:28).

8. NOT FORGOTTEN

Genesis Chapter Eight, Verse One.
"And God remembered Noah, and every living thing, and all the cattle that was with him in the ark: and God made a wind to pass over the earth, and the waters asswaged."

"God remembered Noah." Because there have been periods of time in our experiences when we did not have a direct word from the Lord, it did not mean that He had forgotten us. Neither had God forgotten Noah. It is only that God's plans and purposes often take time to work into the right place and position. With Noah it was taking time for the judgments of the Lord to have their full effect. The judgment had not only come to destroy the wicked, but much time was taken in cleansing the earth of every vestige of evil man's work. No, it was not that Noah had been forgotten. Rather, the Lord was making preparation for Noah's future, and not only his, but the future of all who would follow after him. We also have that thought in "He hath remembered his covenant." This was repeated by Mary in the song she sang: The Magnificat. Then we have the words of Zacharias when he said, "To perform the mercy promised to our father, and remember his holy covenant" (Luke 1:54, 72).

There is not one word that God has spoken in any promise that He will fail to fulfill. All will be fulfilled. He will remember. Not as though He had forgotten and then suddenly remembered what He had said, but His plans and His purposes have to be wrought out on the anvil of time. So if you are waiting for the word of God to be fulfilled, remember, He has not forgotten you. "Cast not away therefore your confidence, which hath great recompence of reward. For ye have need of patience, that, after ye have done the will of God, ye might receive the promise. For yet a little while, and he that shall come will come, and will not tarry. Now the just shall live by faith" (Heb. 10:35-38).

9. BOUNTIFUL BLESSINGS

Genesis Chapter Nine, Verse One.
"And God blessed Noah and his sons, and said unto them, Be fruitful, and multiply, and replenish the earth."

The blessings of God are multiple and varied. Noah was blessed in that he and his family had been saved from the judgment; not only saved, but also kept by the power and the wisdom of God. Through all the time that they had spent inside the ark, there had been the blessings of God in the restraint upon the animals and all other creatures. Then there had been the miracle of supply. The miracle of fresh air. The miracle of sanitation. There was no doubt about it that God had already blessed Noah in the ark, but here again the word declares with strong emphasis, "And God blessed Noah and his sons." There are so many blessings that we as believers receive, they are innumerable, and like the song we sing:

> Count your many blessings;
> Name them one by one,
> And it will surprise you,
> What the Lord hath done.

The psalmist says, "Blessed be the Lord, who daily loadeth us with benefits" (Ps. 68:19). There are times when we have areas of special blessing —the extra, the particular. Because so many of the blessings of God are always there they do not seem very special; but there comes the time of the unexpected, the unusual. "God blessed."

With the blessing, there comes to Noah new commitments and new responsibilities. "Be fruitful, and multiply, and replenish the earth." It was to be a new beginning. It was the repetition of the command and commission that was first given to Adam. "And God blessed them, and God said unto them, be fruitful and multiply, and replenish the earth" (Gen. 1:28). Noah was to re-people the earth with a new generation that would serve the Lord.

This is the calling of every born-again believer. To multiply, to be fruitful, and to tell others of the love and mercy of God that they may be saved, and they in turn may tell still others. Then shall we know indeed the blessing of God in our lives. He blesses us that we may bless others, and then we in return are once again blessed.

10. CONTINUING RECORDS

Genesis Chapter Ten, Verse One.
"Now these are the generations of the sons of Noah, Shem, Ham, and Japheth: and unto them were sons born after the flood."

God keeps perfect records and nothing that really matters for the purpose of the account is missing. Noah had fulfilled the plan of God. He had preached the word of judgment. He had prepared a place of safety. He had delivered himself and his family, and now he propagates his kind. To fulfill the Word of God there must be the bringing forth, the going forth, and the multiplying. This must ever be the vision of the church. Not only must we be satisfied to rest in the ark of salvation (Christ), but there must be a going forth, and the spreading of the truth that there is still room for more. A startling passage of Scripture is the one in Luke 14:16-22 where the supper had been made and invitations had gone out freely to all who would come, without regard to status or standing, and at the end of it all it was said by the servants, "Lord, it is done as thou hast commanded, *and yet there is room.*"

Just as the family of Noah did not die out after the flood, but "sons were born unto them after the flood," so it is after Calvary. Although to the world at large, to the eyes of natural man, Christ was dead, His disciples scattered, the cause of the Kingdom apparently overthrown, actually Christ was alive, and after Calvary "sons were born." On the Day of Pentecost, three thousand were born on one day. A little later on, there were five thousand, and later still, multitudes, and a great multitude. Then we read that there were added to the church daily such as should be saved. So today the propagating still goes on. The records are being kept in heaven, and one day the full "generation of Jesus the Savior" will be written. Christ will be the writer, and it will be called "The Lamb's Book of Life." It will be the complete list of the sons that were born. Until that day, we must go forward and tell the world that their names can be written among the generation of the sons of God.

11. ONE SPEECH

Genesis Chapter Eleven, Verse One.
"And the whole earth was of one language, and of one speech."

What! No language barrier? Perfect unity in conveying thought was indeed a wonderful thing. It is only as you have traveled in different lands where you have not been able to speak the language that you can really appreciate the meaning of this statement: "The whole earth was of one language, and of one speech." Just think how it would be if everyone that you turned to understood what you said—not merely the words, but the intentions. This was the perfect will of God. But owing to the fact that men decided to stay right there in Shinar instead of fulfilling the word of God and replenishing the earth, God had to cause them to scatter abroad and to cease their project of building the city and tower of Babel, as it was later called. Thus there were new languages given by the miraculous intervention of God. So the purpose of God was fulfilled in the replenishing of the earth. The nations were formed, each with its own language. From that time to this day, this has formed a barrier between peoples and nations to some degree. Men have tried to overcome the barrier of language time and time again. There have been attempts at forming a world language, one language for all people. Men will fail to do this, for it is God who brought about the cofusion of languages and it will be God who will also cause the confusion to cease in His plan and at His time. There is going to be a day when once again we will all speak the same language. For then the preaching of the gospel will cease, because its purpose will have been fulfilled. The earth in its new sphere will have one language, one tongue. "For then will I turn to the people a pure language, that they may all call upon the name of the Lord, to serve him with one consent" (Zeph. 3:9; see also Rev. 7:9-12; 20:12-15; 21:1-5; and 22:1-3).

12. EVADING THE CALL

Genesis Chapter Twelve, Verse One.
"Now the Lord had said unto Abram,
Get thee out of thy country, and from
thy kindred, and from thy father's house,
unto a land that I will shew thee."

There was no mistaking the direction of the Lord. It was clear, precise, and easily understood. From the first statement, it is evident that the Lord had spoken to Abram before this time that we read of in chapter 12. What is recorded in chapter 12 through chapter 13 verse 18 is what Abram had to endure while being out of the will of God. Much more of this period of Abram's life is covered in chapter 11 verses 31-33.

The word "had" in the opening sentence gives to us the clue, for this gives the whole of the direction of the Lord a backward look, being in the past tense. It is evident from chapter 11 verse 31 and 32 that Abram did not obey the Lord, and it was not Abram that led the way, but Terah, the father of Abram. The command had been " . . . from thy father's house, from thy kindred." Was it that Abram thought to do the will of God after the death of his father? Had he thought that God's timing of the call to leave all was inopportune, and not at a convenient time? However that may be, he had put it off to a later day. This is surely one of the devil's greatest weapons against the believer, the church, and the sinner—to procrastinate, to put off. There will be time later, says the adversary, and it will be more fitting, a more convenient time. What a seemingly reasonable argument. Your father is old, and to leave him now, Abram, would be no testimony of your love to God or to your neighbors. So he did not do what he should have done when he was called to do it. We must ever watch this aspect of our Christian life. There will be that which we will miss by not obeying the Lord and His word promptly. The Lord said to Abram, "Get thee out," and the word in the Hebrew is in the imperative tense. So what God had said to Abram was, "Abram, get thee out *now*." As we have already said, we miss so much by not doing what the Lord asks of us, when He requires it.

Some years ago I learned that if we don't do what the Lord wants us to do, He will find someone else to do it. The result is that the work is done just the same, but we lose the blessing that could have been ours. It was during one morning while I was at work. The Lord spoke very clearly to me, and told me to take a certain sum of money to a certain person. Now I was listening well and going along with the Lord fine, until He mentioned the name of the person. Straightway when the man's name came, I said, "Lord, he doesn't need this money, he has more money that I have. Lord, You know he has a business downtown, and everyone knows that he is not without money." So I reasoned myself out of what God wanted me to do. I was able to get home for my mid-day meal and did not mention any of the matter to my wife. Later in the day, back at work, the whole matter had been forgotten by me, of course. But not by the Lord. That evening when I came home, my wife said to me, "What do you think the Lord said to me this afternoon?" I replied, "Well, I don't know." She said that the Lord had spoken to her and told her to take a certain sum of money to a certain person. It was the same sum of money and the same person. When I asked her what she had done, she said she had taken it along and found that the man needed the money, that in spite of all that was showing outside, with his business and his position, that he needed the money for a particular need. So from that incident I learned that if I don't do what God wants me to do, He will find someone else to do it. Also, if it is a matter of material things, He knows how to get it out of the same purse, and the will of God is done, and I lose the blessing of doing it.

It was a blind step for Abram to take, to leave the tangible and all he knew and loved to go into the unknown. One thing was sure, he had the promise of God. If you will notice, there were three things that God asked him to leave, and in return God gave him eight things. He had to leave his country, his father's house, and his kindred. In return he was promised a new land, a new nation, a personal blessing, a great name, a source of blessing, a reciprocal blessing, a reciprocal curse and blessing, and a world-propagated blessing.

So in faith Abram later went forth at the command of God, but not before he had seen the folly of not obeying the Lord sooner. Let us do His will whatever the circumstances may be when He calls us to obey.

34

God knows the best
  And although it be a test,
To do His will is not for our ill,
  For God alone knows best.

13. UP AND OUT

Genesis Chapter Thirteen, Verse One.
"And Abram went up out of Egypt, he, and
his wife, and all that he had, and Lot
with him into the south."

Abram, in the first place, had no right to go down
into Egypt. By going down into Egypt he was dis-
obeying to known will of God. When once we
know what we ought to do, and are not doing it,
there is no knowing where we will go, or what we
will do. Abram lied concerning Sarai, his wife, and
put her in danger. So we do not only endanger our
own lives in our backsliding, but the lives of
others, also. It is good to know that Abram "went
up and out." It is always an upward move when we
get right with the Lord. Later, we read in the same
chapter in verse 14, the Lord said unto him, "Lift
up thine eyes." So first he came up, and afterwards
he looked up. There is a divine order here if we can
see it. When he came out of Egypt, it was not long
before he was able to do the whole will of God with
a willing heart. He decided that it was not only out
of Egypt, but out from his kindred, as the Lord
had before commanded him in Genesis 12:1. This
was the beginning of the blessing of the Lord upon
the life of Abram. So it will be with us. All our
blessings begin with complete obedience to the
Word of the Lord.

14. IT HAPPENED AGAIN

Genesis Chapter Fourteen, Verse One.
"And it came to pass in the days of Amraphel king of Shinar, Arioh king of Ellasar, Chedorlaomer king of Elam, and Tidal king of nations."

This is an oft-repeated word in the Scriptures "And it came to pass." Whatever it is that happens, God has it all under His watchful eye and under His control. There is not one thing that ever escapes His observations. "His eye goeth to and fro, He seeth both the evil and the good." So we can assuredly say, "He knoweth the way that I take." Whether it be in the days of the kings who are wicked rulers, or of the kings that are good rulers, the Lord will cause everything ultimately to work out right for us. "For we know that all things work together for good to them that love God, to them who are the called according to his purpose" (Rom. 8:28). So whether it is kings, presidents, or governments that rule, He rules over them all, and He will work everything out for the good of His people and His kingdom.

15. NOTHING STOPS

Genesis Chapter Fifteen, Verse One.
"After these things the word of the Lord came unto Abram in a vision, saying, Fear not, Abram: I am thy shield, and thy exceeding great reward."

After what things? The defeat of the three kings; the rescue of Lot, his nephew; the fellowship with the king of Salem, Melchizedek; the refusing of the offer of the king of Sodom; and the lifting up of the heart and the hand to the Most High God.

It had been a time of strenuous activity. Great demands had been made upon Abram. There had been the physical demands in the war against the kings. There had been the emotional demands in seeking to save Lot, his nephew, out of captivity. There had been also the carnal demands as the king of Sodom offered all the wealth to him. Then there had been the spiritual demands and in return he had worshiped with Melchizedek, the priest of God, and had given him tithes.

So, after these things God came with His Word. When we take our stand for righteousness and truth, and when the battle is over, the time for review comes—it is then that God will come to us. He comes that He might strengthen us, encourage us, and refresh us with the assurance of His presence and His promises for the future. Could it have been that in the mind of Abram there was a fear of reprisals from the three kings? For after all, Abram had but 318 men, and what were they? Yet God had given to him the victory—but now to sit down and think it all out! So God came to him, with His great promise, "Fear not, Abram, I am thy shield." First of all the Lord dispelled all his fears.

Many of God's people need to know that He does not want us to have any fear at all. Fear is from the adversary of our soul. It is the very opposite of faith. "God hath not given us the spirit of fear, but of power, and of love, and of a sound mind" (2 Tim. 1:7). It is then that the Lord gives to Abram the promise of protection, "I am thy shield." Now, you cannot altogether win a battle with a shield, but you can be saved from wounds and from death. So the Lord was saying to Abram, I will protect you, and save you from all hurt and harm, and keep you from death. We read a great deal in the Word of God about God being our shield and defense. There is the shield of faith in Ephesians: "Above all taking the shield of faith, whereby ye shall be able to quench all the fiery darts of the wicked one" (Eph. 6:16). Just to think of the Lord being our shield will remove all our fears. To use the shield of faith will protect us from every evil thing. His name is our shield, the name of *Jesus*.

Then, although Abram had not taken any material gain from the king of Sodom, the Lord said unto him, I am your gain—"I am thy exceeding great reward." God used superlatives here. *To exceed* means "going beyond." What the Lord had really said to Abram was, I will be to you far beyond the greatest reward that you could ever receive from men. Thus we can see that for us, when the storm is

39

over, when you are through with the fight, when you feel that you have given all and received nothing in return—God still *is*! He is our Shield, our Defense, our Helper, and above all, He is our exceeding great reward.

16. BARRENNESS OR BIRTHS

Genesis Chapter Sixteen, Verse One.
"Now Sarai Abram's wife bare him no children: and she had an handmaid, an Egyptian, whose name was Hagar."

To bear no children was the worst thing that could happen to any wife in the days when Abram lived. Barrenness was considered a curse. It caused the heart to cry out. Abram had already spoken to the Lord concerning this barrenness: "Lord God, what wilt thou give me, seeing I go childless?" (Gen. 15:2). Abram had asked for children, fertility, fruitfulness, and seed of his own. The Lord had said that He was his reward.

This should surely be the cry of the church: Give us children. Give us souls. Make us fertile, to bring forth of like kind. Are we condemned by the lack of our desire, by being satisfied in possessing life for ourselves alone? To possess life and not to give life is to die. Certain plants have both flowers and fruits at the same time, and as long as you keep picking the fruit, they will bring forth more bountifully. Leave the fruit, and the flowers bloom and fall. The more life we give to others, the more we have to give. So let us not be content with our barrenness, but cry unto the Lord for more fruitfulness of life.

There had to be a change both in Sarai and in Abram. Their names give to us an insight into their nature, and their characters are revealed. *Sarai* means "contentious, quarrelsome." She saw in everyone else what she inwardly desired and she turned it into criticism and openly chided others about it. That is why she looked at Hagar and made the plans she did, then acted upon them. But her purpose being accomplished brought great hurt and bitterness. She needed a change from that contentious spirit. That kind of spirit will never bring forth or bare. The name *Abram* means "lofty father." This points to a cause of barrenness also. *Lofty* surely speaks of pride of heart. This pride had to go. What a way to be rid of pride! Here he was with a most beautiful wife, but her a barren woman—what a reproach this was to him! When pride had been dealt with in the failure of Hagar's child being accepted by the Lord as the seed of Abram, and the contentious spirit was challenged by the heavenly messengers, then came not only the new names, but the new attitudes. The result was fruitfulness. Lord, evermore keep us from a contentious and a proud spirit.

17. NO LIMITS WITH GOD

> *Genesis Chapter Seventeen, Verse One.*
> "And when Abram was ninety years old and nine, the Lord appeared to Abram, and said unto him, I am the Almighty God; walk before me, and be thou perfect."

The one thing that stands out among others here is the age of Abram. No matter what the number of years are, whether it be the boyish years of Samuel, or the ninety-nine years of Abram, God still appears, and still speaks to hearts and minds. How often the believer thinks in terms of being too young or too old. We are neither too young nor too old for the Lord to reveal Himself to us. When we shut ourselves into an age bracket, we are just as surely shutting up our ears, as though we were deaf. We do not hear the Lord simply because we are not listening. The reason is that we have come to believe that God only speaks to a certain age group, and so we do not expect Him to speak to us.

The revelation that the Lord gave to Abram was new to man. When He said to Abram, "I am Almighty God," He was saying, I am El Shaddai, the God of *"all sufficiency!"* He was assuring Abram that there could never be a need in his life, whether it was in his body, spirit, or soul, that could not be met by God. When he needed strength, the Lord would be that strength. Although Abram had received the promise of a son, he was still in a state of doubting. He needed more assurances, and the Lord gave them to him in this all inclusive name of *Shaddai*.

"Walk before me, and be thou perfect." The Word of God has a lot to say about "our walk." So often we miss the real significance of "before me." We are concerned with our walk before men, which of course is important, but not half as important as walking before the Lord. We can walk before men, be seen and be heard, in such a way as to be thought well of; but we can never deceive the Lord. What a lack is revealed in us when we think that we can act or speak without God seeing or knowing all. It is reasonable to see why the Lord added, "and be thou perfect." *Perfection* is a frightening word to most of us. The first thought that it brings is, no mistakes, no need for correction. But that is not the meaning of the word as used here at all. The word here, as in many other places in the Hebrew means, "upright and sincere." *Uprightness* and *sincerity* speak of "righteousness," "rightness," "no known wrong." If we couple this with walking with God, and walking before the Lord, we can be recipients of God's fullness and covenant. Let us do, let us be, all things in the light of this knowledge, that nothing is hid from the Lord.

18. THE UNEXPECTED

Genesis Chapter Eighteen, Verse One.
"And the Lord appeared unto him in the
plains of Mamre: and he sat in the tent
door in the heat of the day."

The unexpected that can happen in a day! The
rest period! The heat of the day! There is much for
our thoughts here today. God in the unexpected.
Our thoughts are on the past and we have been
dwelling on the things that have been. We are
thinking of our failures, our successes, the trials,
and also the things that might have been otherwise. Suddenly, God breaks in. We see Him, we
hear Him, we know that it is He, and we forget
everything—even the rest, the heat of the day is
forgotten, for ourselves, yes, but not for Him. We
worship, we minister to Him. This is one of the
greatest needs that the Lord has, the need for His
people to stop a while and worship Him. To think
of God as having any need at all seems unreal and
not the truth; but Jesus Himself said, "But the hour
cometh, and now is, when the true worshippers
shall worship the Father in spirit and in truth: for
the Father seeketh such to worship him." Today you
may be compelled to rest because of "the heat of the
day"—rest because of sickness, infirmity, or problems, and you are hiding from that heat in the tent
door. Then He comes. You didn't expect Him. You
were filled with your own need. You saw Him, and
in your spirit knew that He was passing by and

would be gone unless you did something. You forgot everything of yourself, and you rose up to meet Him. It was first out of your own need to lay hold on Him so that He would not pass by you. Had Abram not risen up to meet Him, the Lord would have possibly passed on to do that which He was on His way to accomplish. So it was that Abram intreated, and the Lord fellowshiped with him, and worship was given. Let us today look for Him in the unexpected, though we are resting from the heat of the day.

The unexpected.
  The rest.
    The heat of the day.
      The visitation of the Lord.
        The worship from his own.

19. DIVINE INTERVENTION

Genesis Chapter Nineteen, Verse One.
"And there came two angels to Sodom at even; and Lot sat in the gate of Sodom: and Lot seeing them rose up to meet them; and he bowed himself with his face toward the ground."

What a great similarily between this verse and the verse of the previous chapter. But there is a difference—one is far removed from the other. Abram was sitting in his tent door. It was in the plains of Mamre, and it was in the heat of the day. Lot sat in the gate of the city at even. Lot had made his choice earlier. He had chosen the well-watered plains of Sodom. The immediate outlook was the best and the way to it was the easiest, but it had the most temptations. We must always be on the alert and be aware of taking the line of least resistance. It may not be good for us in the end.

There were six steps that Lot took before we find him established in the city of wickedness. *He strove* (Gen. 13:7); *he beheld* (Gen. 13:10); *he chose* (Gen. 13:7, 10-12); *he pitched toward* (Gen. 13:12); *he dwelt in* (Gen. 14:12); *he sat in the gate* (Gen. 19:1). As far as the material things and his social position with men is concerned, he had risen and was now counted as an elder, a counselor, and in this position he sat in the gate of the city in the evening. The heavenly visitation, too, was on a different basis than the visitation to Abram. The visit to Abram was for fellowship. The visit to Lot was for warning. How blind Lot was to his own position. How near to destruction he was at that moment. How ignorant was his mind to the condition and sinfulness of the city of Sodom. It is true that it is recorded that he didn't like the acts of the men of Sodom (2 Peter 2:6-8). Yet although he was vexed and disturbed within himself, he was content with his position, and sat as one of them, with them in the gate of the city. May the Spirit of God ever warn us of the dangers of unseemly prosperity.

Abram had gained a victory over the three kings, then had refused the gains that the king of Sodom offered him. Was it possible that Lot had taken full advantage of this? Had the king of Sodom given much to Lot because of Abram's victory for them? Did the people of Sodom accept Lot because his uncle Abram delivered them out of the hands of the three kings? Was the temptation too big for Lot? At any rate, he became as one of them. He enjoyed the possessions they gave to him, but he could never really enjoy their fellowship. He enjoyed his position, but he could not change their ways. Compromise never wins for Christ. To outwardly show agreement one needs only to "sit in the gate." "Blessed is the man that *walketh not* in the counsel of the ungodly; *nor standeth* in the way of sinners; *not sitteth* in the seat of the scornful" (Ps. 1:1).

Let us make sure why we are permitted to have a heavenly visitation. Is it for fellowship and blessing—or is it for warning and deliverance? Lot was to reap the harvest at a later time.

20.   GOING ON TOWARD?

Genesis Chapter Twenty, Verse One.
"And Abraham journeyed from thence
toward the south country, and dwelled
between Kadesh and Shur, and sojourned
in Gerar."

What was it in the journeying toward the south
that caused Abraham to be ensnared in the lies of
deception? It was exactly the same story repeated
from Genesis 12:9. Going south, the same deception, from the same kind of fear. One thing which
seems to stand out from this portion is that, seeing
Abraham was afraid, and because he remembered
the past experience, he would have done well to
have kept from going south altogether, unless he
was able to go in the fear of the Lord, and with truth
on his lips. In all our journeyings through our
Christian life, unless we have the victory in our
hearts and lives, we had better keep away from that
which would make us live a lie. We must not pre-
sume upon the grace of God to keep us if we cannot
keep ourselves from the lie. Jesus said to the devil,
"Thou shalt not tempt the Lord thy God" (Luke
4:12). Jesus surely had been promised "He shall
give his angels charge over thee" (Luke 4:10). Jesus
was asked of the devil to prove something—"that
you are the Son of God." We do not have to prove
what we are, let alone run into danger to prove it.
Joseph in the house of Potiphar did not try to prove
that he was stronger than other men. No! He ran

away from that which he could have been ensnared in. It is better to run than to ruin. Let us watch our walk and remember what caused us to fail in past days. Let us keep aware of this. It is better that we be called "chicken" now, than to fail, and later to be called "foul."

> Dare to be a Daniel;
>   Dare to stand alone,
> Dare to have a purpose true,
>   And dare to make it known.

21. FULFILLMENT

Genesis Chapter Twenty-one, Verse One.
"And the Lord visited Sarah as he had said, and the Lord did unto Sarah as he had spoken."

God always keeps His word. The covenants that He makes are sure covenants. He never at any time has broken His word. Should a promise be given to an individual, then that individual will see the fulfilled word. The time of testing is the time from His speaking until the time of His performing the promise. With the Lord, time is as nothing. But to the one who is waiting, it seems as an eternity. We have need of patience after we have received the promise.

Twice in Genesis 18 the Lord said to Sarah, "I will return unto thee." Looking at it from the natural order, it was an impossibility for her to have a child, and then as the time extended, the impossibility increased. Each year, each *day*, it grew more difficult to believe. But God had spoken, and that was enough. He had made the promise, and as far as He was concerned, the work was done. So at all times we must recognize His word as final, and be assured that He will visit us as He has declared. Faith is ours, but *fulfillment is His*.

22. STILL MORE TO COME

Genesis Chapter Twenty-two, Verse One.
"And it came to pass after these things,
that God did tempt Abraham, and said
unto him, Abraham: and he said, Behold,
here I am."

"After these things." There will be no end of
things that the Lord will do for us if we are ready for
Him to speak to us. Up to this moment in the life of
Abraham it had been one test after another, and
now he has settled down to enjoy his son, Isaac, the
God-fulfilled promise and faith's reward. Time has
slipped by, Hagar and Ishmael have been sent
away; Isaac remains. The son of promise is there,
and he is the center of all their devotion. Just when
it seems that the blessing of the Lord cannot get any
better than they are now enjoying, God speaks.
There is ever present with us the danger of being so
taken up with the temporal blessings that we cannot hear when the Lord speaks to us. Can it be that
we become so satisfied with things as they are that
we do not want Him to speak lest He would have
new demands for us to fill? Abraham did not know
that it was a test. But how quick he is to hear, and
how quickly he responds. "Behold, here I am." No
matter how great our blessings, let them never dull
our hearing for His voice. May the suggestion
never enter our hearts that the Lord wants to rob us
or to take from us that which He has given us. Love
only gives, and asks that it might receive more love

in return, so that more shall be given again to the giver. It is a great privilege to be tested by the Lord. Smith Wigglesworth once said, "The best thing that you could ever have is a great trial. It is your robing time. It is coming into your inheritance. Voice your position and you will be surrounded by all the resources of God in time of trial." These words, "God did test Abraham," are full of dignity. There are no words in the Bible that say, "And God did test Lot." May we be kept from becoming so preoccupied that we cannot hear when the Lord speaks to us. I pray that the Lord will keep us from loving our present possessions, whether it be things or people, too much, so that we do not hear His voice.

23. THE FAITHFUL GOD

Genesis Chapter Twenty-three, Verse One.
"And Sarah was an hundred and seven and twenty years old: these were the years of the life of Sarah."

The insignificant becomes the significant when it has been recorded in the Word of God. The ordinary becomes important when we realize that "all scripture is given by the inspiration of God, and is profitable for doctrine, for reproof, for correction, for instruction in righteousness, that the man of God may be perfect, thoroughly furnished unto all good works" (2 Tim. 3:16-17). We ask ourselves, what can we profit from the record of Sarah's age? Is there anything of reproof, doctrine, correction, or instruction? Well, first of all let us realize that God keeps good records. There is the Book of Life (Rev. 20:15). There is the Book of Remembrance (Mal. 3:16). There is the Book of the Lord (Isa. 34:16). The books were opened (Rev. 20:12).

But why Sarah's age? First there is the record of God's faithfulness to His word of promise. She was able to bear Isaac in her old age, and raise him to manhood before she died. God will fulfill His word to those to whom He has spoken, and then leave enough time to rejoice in its fulfillment, no matter how long or how short that time may be. Secondly, it leaves us in no doubt as to the miracle of the birth of Isaac. Sarah was ninety years and more at the time of the birth of Isaac (Gen. 17:17). The apostle Paul speaks of the deadness of Sarah's womb (Rom. 4:19). The record has it, "Now Abraham and Sarah were old and well stricken in age, and it ceased to be with Sarah after the manner of women" (Gen. 18:11). After the birth of Isaac she lived on another twenty-seven years to enjoy the promise. So, no matter how difficult our case, or how long we have waited, the record will later say, God kept His word and gave life over and above the promise given. If we have doubted, here is proof for us. If we have thought our case and our position impossible, here is correction, knowing all that happened to Sarah. The record then becomes our instruction: "Now all these things happened unto them for ensamples; and they are written for our admonition, upon whom the ends of the world are come" (1 Cor. 10:11).

24. FULLNESS IN ALL THINGS

Genesis Chapter Twenty-four, Verse One.
"And Abraham was old, and well stricken in age: and the Lord had blessed Abraham in all things."

What a testimony to the faithfulness of God! Since the day that Abraham had left his kindred and his country, and had gone forward trusting the word of God, there had been trials and tests, and even failure on his part—but the Lord had not failed him in one promise. He had blessed him in all things. The covenants that God had made to Abraham were without conditions. Many of the promises to God's people are conditional, but in these made to Abraham conditions are not attached. When we see the utter shortcomings of the descendants of Abraham, we can well understand the covenant that the Lord Himself made with Abraham. Had there been a condition, then the Lord would have only extended the covenant to Abraham and Isaac. Here is one of the great mysteries of the mercy of God in His foreknowledge.

There are many blessings that we do not deserve, but we receive them just the same. Is it not because of His Son? "For Jesus' sake," is indeed a cry that can come from the lips and the hearts of God's erring children. The ten lepers asked only for mercy. The Syrophenician woman asked for crumbs that fell from the table, and she got perfect healing for her daughter. The thief on the cross could not present one qualifying claim for any good that he had done. He asked only to be remembered in the Kingdom. He received there and then just what the other saints in paradise had.

"O the depth of the riches both of the wisdom and knowledge of God! how unsearchable are his judgments, and his ways past finding out! For who hath known the mind of the Lord? or who hath been his counsellor? Or who hath first given to him, and it shall be recompensed unto his again? For of him, and through him, and to him, are all things: to whom be glory for ever. Amen" (Rom. 11:33-36).

25. DIVINE RENEWAL

Genesis Chapter Twenty-five, Verse One.
"Then again Abraham took a wife, and her name was Keturah."

It is remarkable that after we have read that Abraham was old and well stricken in age that this verse should follow. It tells us that although Sarah had died, and Isaac was there, Abraham did not give up living, but he rose up again, even in his old age, to live the best he knew how. The record of his life with Keturah is only a short one, but it tells us he had six more sons. There should be enough encouragement here for us that no matter what happens in our life faith and grace is given to rise up again and go on. So often the shores of time are littered with the wrecks of lives that have failed to rise again and go forward. The storm came into their lives, they were beaten and tossed about, they had no will to go forward again, and the frail vessel of human nature just let the waves of circumstances continually roll over them until it seems that there was no possible hope of recovery. The will to live and to bless and be blessed is before us all. We live now in time, we must make all the use of it we can, for time passes on and is no more. In eternity, the endless ages, we shall know the reasons why. What we have failed to understand here we shall fully understand there. So let us take courage and hope, and let faith rise today that, no matter what our experience has been, we can rise up and begin a new life with Him.

Let us consider one more thought. The name *Keturah* means "fragrance." As with Abraham, so all that is past, whether it is success, failure, disappointment, old age, or whatever there has been, we can begin a new life of fragrance, and spiritually we can bring forth fruit in old age.

"The righteous shall flourish like the palm tree: he shall grow like a cedar in Lebanon. Those that be planted in the house of the Lord shall flourish in the courts of our God. They shall still bring forth fruit in old age; they shall be fat and flourishing; to shew that the Lord is upright: he is my rock, and there is no unrighteousness in him" (Ps. 92:12-15).

26. LIKE FATHER—LIKE SON

Genesis Chapter Twenty-six, Verse One.
"And there was a famine in the land,
beside the first famine that was in the days
of Abraham. And Isaac went unto
Abimelech king of the Philistines unto
Gerar."

History so often repeats itself. So as to leave us
with no doubts, here is the record of another time of
need. It is now Isaac the son rather than Abraham
the father who has to face the same kind of situation.

It is the hardest thing to do, just to stay right where
we are when trouble or difficulty comes our way.
The nature of man makes him want to get away from
the hard way to an easier way. Naomi and Elimelech
left Bethlehem Judah in a time of famine. Later, on
her return, Naomi confessed, "I went out full, and I
returned empty." We can be full in time of famine
and empty in the time of plenty. There are very few
lives that have constant trouble or constant ease.
Surely the one is set against the other, and, I am
persuaded, this is for our benefit. "In the day of
prosperity be joyful, but in the day of adversity consider: God also hath set the one over against the
other, to the end that man should find nothing after
him" (Eccles. 7:14). "If thou faint in the day of
adversity, thy strength is small" (Prov. 24:10).

One thing seems sure, that when the famine comes we should not go down to Egypt (the world) for our help. He who has blessed us in prosperity will keep us in the famine. It is better to have fellowship with God in the famine than to have plenty with the unsaved in Egypt but no communion with God. The promise of God is sure, "Our bread and water shall be sure." God had fairly proportioned out the night and the day. So let us not start running away when trouble comes, but rather start reigning in it.

When we see others in a test or a trial, let us beware of prejudging or of saying what we would do if we were in the same place. We cannot tell what we would do under the same conditions. "For that ye ought to say, If the Lord will, we shall live, and do this, or that. But now ye rejoice in your boastings: all such rejoicing is evil" (James 4:15-16). There seems to be a general principle that that which befalls one comes to another in some degree. So we need to take heed to the exhortation of the Word of God, "There hath no temptation taken you but such as is common to man: but God is faithful, who will not suffer you to be tempted above that ye are able; but will with the temptation also make a way to escape, that ye may be able to bear it" (1 Cor. 10:13). "Therefore judge nothing before the time, until the Lord come, who both will bring to light the hidden things of darkness, and will make manifest the counsels of the hearts: and then shall every man have praise of God" (1 Cor. 4:5). So let us each day walk before the Lord in humility of heart, knowing what happens to another by the law of reoccurrence could happen to us; and in such humility, let us pray one for another.

27. PARENTAL RESPONSIBILITY

Genesis Chapter Twenty-seven, Verse One.
"And it came to pass, that when Isaac was old, and his eyes were dim, so that he could not see, he called Esau his oldest son, and said unto him, My son: and he said unto him, Behold, here am I."

Old age need not necessarily take away the sense of responsibility. The person who has lived for God, and has been actively engaged not only physically but also in the spiritual realm, will remain alive and alert in the things of the Spirit, although the natural forces are slowed down. Here we see that Isaac was old. He could not see, but he knew that he had an obligation to fulfill in that, as the head of his family, he had to pass on to the eldest son the blessing of his fatherly hands and words. This was actually the endorsement of the birthright. This naturally belonged to Esau, but the divine plan and purpose had already been revealed to his mother, and the promise of the birthright was already promised to Jacob.

Could it be that Isaac was not only blind physically, but also blind spiritually? Had he not been informed by his wife Rebekah? Or had he let his idolizing of Esau, and his love for venison, take away the sense of spiritual values? Could he not see that Esau had no real desire for the things of the

Spirit? Could he not see that Esau thought only of prestige and power?

No matter how many years we have passed in the natural realm, we must always keep in touch with God and the things of the Spirit. When we lean too much to things of the natural life, we are in danger of becoming blinded to spiritual realities, and our senses will become dulled, so that we will not discern between good and evil. There are so many things that God would tell us, if only He could get us to listen. "Of whom we have many things to say, and hard to be uttered, seeing ye are dull of hearing. For when for the time ye ought to be teachers, ye have need that one teach you again which be the first principles of the oracles of God; and are become such as have need of milk, and not of strong meat. For every one that useth milk is unskilful in the word of righteousness: for he is a babe. But strong meat belongeth to them that are of full age, even those who by reason of use *have their senses exercised to discern both good and evil*" (Heb. 5:11-14).

Let us not be as Isaac, with our mind so filled with the natural order of things that we cannot discern the spiritual order. After many years of seeing and hearing, he did not know God's plan.

28. SEPARATION

*Genesis Chapter Twenty-eight, Verse
One.*
"And Isaac called Jacob, and blessed him,
and charged him, and said unto him, Thou
shalt not take a wife of the daughters of
Canaan."

The importance of separation was behind the
charge given to Jacob by his father that he was not
to take a wife from the Canaanites. This was not a
matter of family or tribal pride, it was more far-
reaching than personal choice. God's purpose was
for His people to be a separate people unto Him,
and each time this line of separation had been
broken down, the result was confusion and finally
a forsaking of God for other gods. You see this in
Genesis 6:2; where the spiritual line of Seth broke
the line of separation as they took the daughters of
men for their wives. Each time this has happened,
the record left to us is clear. Solomon, unto whom
the Lord had given of His wisdom in great measure, and unto whom came other rulers to see the
greatness of his kingdom and to hear of his wisdom, is an example. It was on this very thing that
he fell and caused the work of God and the people
of God to suffer loss later, when he took to himself
many strange women of other nations. This charge
of Isaac to Jacob is something that is seen right
through the entire Word of God. When we come to
New Testament teaching, it is more explicit than

before. "Be ye not unequally yoked together with unbelievers, for what fellowship hath righteousness with unrighteousness, what communion hath light with darkness? . . . for ye are the temple of the living God; as God hath said, I will dwell in them, and walk in them; and I will be their God, and they shall be my people. Wherefore come out from among them, and be ye separate, saith the Lord . . . and I will receive you, and will be a Father unto you, and ye shall be my sons and daughters, saith the Lord Almighty" (2 Cor. 6:14-18).

The shores of time are filled with the wrecks of lives from the ocean of marriages that began with an unequal yoke. The percentage of such marriages that work out right is very small. Let us take heed to Isaac's charge to Jacob. "Thou shalt not take a wife of the daughters of Canaan." Marry! Yes, but the partners must be of like mind, and most of all, for the believer it must be another believer, if we would seek the blessings of God and peace of mind in future years.

29. WE MUST GO ON

Genesis Chapter Twenty-nine, Verse One.
"Then Jacob went on his journey, and came into the land of the people of the east."

Whatever our experience has been, whether it has been good or bad, we must always seek to go on. To Jacob it was to be a journey that for him was full in mixed feelings. Somewhere behind him was an angry brother filled with a murderous intent. There were the thoughts of the father Isaac, thinking of the events of the past few days. Rebekah, the mother, filled with good intentions that had turned to deceit and lies, and finally a fear that compelled her to send her son away, never to see his face again. But Jacob's latest experience was not with his father, his mother, or his brother—it was with God. God had met him and assured him that he was not going out into the unknown alone, for God said to Jacob, "I am with thee, and will keep thee in all places whither thou goest" (Gen. 28:15). "Then Jacob went on." The translation here in the margin of most Bibles is very enlightening. *"Then Jacob lifted up his feet."* On that first day of the journey, had his feet been heavy? Had they dragged on the way? Was the journey an unwilling, doubtful one filled with thoughts of hazards and fears? But now he hears the promise of his God, and he lifts up his feet because his heart is lifted up by the assurance of the promise of God. Whatever the road we are asked to take, whether the way ahead we cannot see, nor know whether it is full of difficulties or blessings, as long as we know that the Lord is with us and He has given us the word of assurance, we can go ahead. We can lift up our feet and go on our journey again. He has said to us, "I will never leave thee, nor forsake thee. So that we may boldly say, The Lord is my helper, and I will not fear what man shall do unto me" (Heb. 13:5-6). So let us rise up, lift up our feet, leave the past behind, and go on our way on our journey into a land of new people, new plans, new purposes—toward the east and the rising of the sun, which foretells of a new day.

30. FRUITFULNESS OR ELSE

Genesis Chapter Thirty, Verse One.
"And when Rachel saw that she bare Jacob no children, Rachel envied her sister; and said unto Jacob, Give me children, or else I die."

Envy is most unreasonable in its demands. Its spreading roots gather nourishment from many sources. For Rachel it was constantly looking at Leah and the children she had been blessed with, whereas Rachel herself had no children and was not able to have any at this time. Was there a cause for her barrenness? Was it in the fact that it was she whom Jacob had loved in the first place? After Jacob had discovered that Leah had been given to him, he left off paying attention to Leah, and Leah in a great measure was forgotten. The Scripture says, "When the Lord saw that Leah was *hated*, he opened her womb and shut Rachel's."

It is a well-known medical fact that hate and envy can cause such tension in the body that a lot of natural functions cannot operate. Envy does not have any honorable principles. It was said of Jesus, "That for envy they had delivered him" (Matt. 27:18). Why? Because He was producing what the people needed, and the scribes and Pharisees could not do the same works. To envy another because of what they have, and you have not, will soon bring you into barrenness. It will also cause you to act in an unreasonable way. The brothers of Joseph "envied him" until, without thinking how far they would go, their intentions were to destroy Joseph. Envy often destroys the thing it wants but cannot attain. Envy and jealousy are closely related. "Wrath is cruel, and anger is outrageous, but who is able to stand before envy?" (Prov. 27:4). "Jealousy is cruel as the grave" (Song of Sol. 8:6). "Jealousy is the rage of man" (Prov. 6:34).

So let us pray that we may be kept from all envy—envy of others in position, envy of others who have possessions—lest we find ourselves like Rachel, making unreasonable demands. "Godliness with contentment is great gain." "For I have learned," said the apostle Paul, "in whatsoever state I am, therewith to be content" (Phil. 4:11).

31. TRANSFERRED GLORY

> *Genesis Chapter Thirty-one, Verse One.*
> "And he heard the words of Laban's sons,
> saying, Jacob hath taken away all that was
> our father's; and of that which was our
> father's hath he gotten all this glory."

To see a change of position come about, the
transfer of power, possessions, and glory, without
knowing the real reason why it has happened, can
be disturbing enough to give a wrong foundation
for wrong actions. How much did the sons of
Laban know about their father's scheming wiles,
the changing of Jacob's wages ten times? How
much did they know about the promise of God to
Jacob? It is far too easy to judge a case by what we
see outwardly. To pass judgment without having
full knowledge is not only unwise, but it is
unrighteous. We must know all the facts before we
speak or act in such matters. There has been many a
person who has been judged on circumstances,
and then for a lifetime has been forced to walk
under a shadow. When we do not know, we should
not speak. We have a direct warning in the Word of
God about such matters and what to do about
"hearsay." So many use the phrase, "I heard," and
then the information is passed on from one person
to another, and a molehill becomes a mountain. "If
thou shalt hear say in one of thy cities . . . then
shalt thou *enquire,* and *make search,* and *ask diligently,* and behold, *if it be truth,* and *the thing certain,*

and that such abomination *is wrought* among you . . ." (Deut. 13:12-14). With the sons of Laban, the truth of the matter was that God had given to Jacob the flocks and the herds (Gen. 31:5-13). So what we hear of others must not be judged without sufficient evidence to confirm the words, otherwise we may find ourselves in the like position as the sons of Laban. Jesus said these words to us all, "Judge not, that ye be not judged, for with what judgment ye judge, ye shall be judged; and with what measure ye mete, it shall be measured to you again" (Matt. 7:1-2).

32. GOING FORWARD TO MEET GOD

Genesis Chapter Thirty-two, Verse One.
"And Jacob went on his way, and the angels of God met him."

As we go forward in our Christian experience, we never know what we are going to meet up with. Here Jacob had a wonderful experience, for as he went forward in his journey he met the angels of God. There is no explanation in the record of why they came. They said no words, and gave no message, but as we look further into the Word of God, we read these wonderful words. "The angel of the Lord encampeth round about them that fear him, and delivereth them" (Ps. 34:7). When Jacob saw those angels, he recognized them and said, "This is God's host." Had they come to reassure him that they were watching over him? He was soon to need that assurance as he heard of Esau and four hundred men coming to meet him. God's host had met him first, like Abraham, who before the king of Sodom met him with the offer of worldly goods, was first met by Melchizedek the priest of the Most High God. There is never a trial that comes our way but what God first of all comes in some way to prepare us and to make us know that He is with us. We have also the words of Jesus, "And when he putteth forth his own sheep, he goeth before them, and the sheep follow him, for they know his voice" (John 10:4). Let us then go forward without fear of what is in the way. Let His way be our way, and let our way be His. As we go forward we shall discover that He will either meet us Himself, or He will send His angels to encourage us.

> God holds the key to all unknown:
>   And I am glad.
> If other hands should hold the key,
> Or if He trusted it to me,
>   I might be sad.
>
> What if tomorrow's cares were here,
>   Without its rest?
> I'd rather He unlocked the day,
> And as the hours swing open say,
>   My will is best.
>
> Enough; this covers all my wants,
>   And so I rest.
> For what I cannot, He can see,
> And in His care I saved shall be,
>   Forever blest.

33. LOOKING—FEAR OR FAITH

Genesis Chapter Thirty-three, Verse One.
"And Jacob lifted up his eyes, and looked, and behold, Esau came, and with him four hundred men. And he divided the children unto Leah, and unto Rachel, and unto the two handmaids."

"And . . . lifted up his eyes and looked." Each time this phrase appears in the Scripture, wherever it was, and whoever it was who lifted up his eyes and looked, it was a look that was to change his life. This is a truth that we need to see if we have not seen it before, and if we know it then to be reminded about it once again. It was Eve who looked toward the forbidden tree, and through that look brought sorrow not only upon herself, but upon the whole world. Abraham lifted up his eyes and saw the ram that was to be the substitute for Isaac, who was to be the forerunner of the Savior. The blind man that Jesus had already touched but who was not fully healed, looked up when Jesus touched him again, and then he saw all men clearly. We need to lift up our eyes that we might see things as they really are. The woman in Luke 13 was earthbound until Jesus loosed her, and then she really saw the sky for the first time for eighteen years. Let us look up, and we will see Him. "I will lift up mine eyes unto the hills," says the psalmist (Ps. 121:1), and he saw God. Too often we are looking too low, and see only the earth. So let us, like Jacob and the rest, lift up our eyes and look, and we shall find God. Jesus said to His disciples, "Lift up your eyes and look on the fields, for they are white already to harvest" (John 4:35). It is the upward look that always changes things. I am always reminded, when I think of looking upward, of the blue hem or fringe that God ordered to be put on the garment of Aaron and his sons. Because blue was the heavenly color, each time they looked down to the earth they saw the hem of blue, and it reminded them to look up. So when the things of the earth get too much for us, let us turn from them and look up, and things will change.

34. BIG DOORS TURN ON LITTLE HINGES

Genesis Chapter Thirty-four, Verse One.
"And Dinah the daughter of Leah, which she bare unto Jacob, went out to see the daughters of the land."

It has been well said that "big doors turn on little hinges." A seemingly ordinary event can turn out to be of great consequence. Two men are talking and one man happens to say the wrong thing, and at the wrong time. An argument begins. The argument gets heated, and it becomes a fight. The fight becomes a family feud, and it has been known in history to become a war between nations. When it is started, who knows where it will end? Only a commonplace event, an unguarded moment, and things begin that were never anticipated. Jacob's daughter was in a strange land. It was all new to her. And so Dinah goes out to see the other young women of this new land. A lonely girl in a strange land. Whatever it was that made her wander alone, curiosity or loneliness, it ended in tragedy for her, for the people of the land, and for Levi and Simeon, her brothers. The unguarded moments are times of decision-making events. In the moments when there is time for leisure or for profit we must watch and be sober. We must fill them with usefulness. Idleness of hand and of mind soon become a snare of the devil, and he will direct our thoughts, which will instruct our hands, and we can become involved in that which is far-reaching, and which could have otherwise been a more profitable time. It is the little foxes that spoil the vines. So often we fail in watching the little things that at the moment seem so unimportant; for instance, the spoken word that is misconstrued. During the years of World War II, everywhere you saw posters that warned all who read that careless talk costs lives. So must we watch the little things of our lives. I think that Peter must have been thinking of such things when he said, "Be sober, be vigilant; because your adversary the devil, as a roaring lion, walketh about, seeking whom he may devour" (1 Peter 5:8).

35. NO SITTING DOWN

Genesis Chapter Thirty-five, Verse One.
"And God said unto Jacob, Arise, go up to
Bethel, and dwell there: and make there an
altar unto God, that appeared unto thee
when thou fleddest from the face of
Esau thy brother."

Arise! God is ever calling His people to rise up.
For Jacob it was to rise up and move his household,
his family, back to the place where God had met
him when he had seemingly no friends behind him
except a fearful mother. Before him loomed the
unknown, the uncertain. It was at Bethel that God
had met him, and had given to him the promise of
His presence. "And behold, I am with thee, and
will keep thee in all places whither thou goest, and
will bring thee again into this land; for I will not
leave thee until I have done that which I have
spoken to thee of" (Gen. 28:15). Here it was that
Jacob had to go with all his family. He was to live
there, and was to make an altar to God right there.
There had to be a putting away of all the other gods
that his people had gathered. Was this one of the
reasons that God was taking him back to Bethel? It
had to be a new day; a new beginning was needed.
The altar had to be made to God—to the God who
had appeared to him at Bethel. Is not this one of the
reasons that we need a revival among the people of
God? A revival is surely a return to the old paths, to
the place where God met us, where He gave to us

the promise of His presence and the assurance of His keeping power. There has been the wandering away, away from the now forgotten experiences of the visitations of God to us in the time we needed His help. For the help came, and the problem of the past has been forgotten in the prosperity of the present, and we have forgotten God in the measure that we have put Him in the background. So often we put God in second place in our worship, and we give other things and people first place. So the call comes—Arise! Let us go back to the God of our beginnings. Back to Bethel. Back to Him who met us when we were without hope or future. Back to Him, who assures us that He will never leave us, that He will keep His word no matter what happens. So let us go, not to visit, but to live there, and build an altar to our God.

> Dwelling in the secret place,
>   Overshadowed by His grace,
> Looking up into His face,
>   Seeing only Jesus.

36. THE ORIGIN OF EVIL

Genesis Chapter Thirty-six, Verse One.
"Now these are the generations of Esau, who is Edom."

It is so easy to forget how things began, and how things originated, and where some people came from in the beginning. With God there is no mistake, for He keeps the records clear, and nothing is omitted so that when the years have slipped by, and we wonder concerning certain people, there is the record of the beginnings. God wanted it on record for all who would inquire about Edom and the Edomites. The Edomites were proud and self-confident (Jer. 49:16). They were strong and cruel (Jer. 49:19). They were of a vindictive nature (Ezek. 25:12). They were idolatrous and also superstitious (2 Chron. 25:12; Jer. 27:3-9). So when we see some of these things in the lives of God's people, and when there is a turning away from the truth, we can find exactly where it all began. It began with a man who despised his birthright and lightly esteemed the inheritance of God. So let us watch when we see pride, self-confidence, cruelty, superstition, or a vindictive spirit—for all these come from the Esau-life. We do not belong to this life when we have been born again. The old life has died on the cross. "We have been crucified with Christ. . . ." We have died with Christ. Having died with Him, we are risen with Him in the newness of life. "If ye then be risen with Christ, seek those things which are above, where Christ sitteth on the right hand of God. Set your affection on things above, not on things on the earth. For ye are dead, and your life is hid with Christ in God" (Col. 3:1-3). Christ has triumphed over Edom for us, that we need no longer be under its dominion (Isa. 63:1-6). The divine record remains to ever warn us and to keep us alert to all the wiles of the adversary, the devil, who never changes. Esau's name is not found among the men of faith in Hebrews 11, but it *is* found in Hebrews 12: "Looking diligently lest any man fail of the grace of God . . . *lest there be any . . . as Esau,* who for one morsel of meat sold his birthright."

37. DWELLING IN THE LAND

Genesis Chapter Thirty-seven, Verse One.
"And Jacob dwelt in the land wherein his father was a stranger, in the land of Canaan."

Time passes so quickly—the years that seemed so far away are soon upon us and before we are aware of it they are passed and are behind us. Jacob was now dwelling in the land of Canaan where his father Isaac had lived and to which his grandfather Abram had come. Not only were they strangers in that land, but they had problems—great problems. In our Christian life we all enjoy in some measure the things that others have striven for and in many cases have also suffered for. We think of the liberty of having God's Word in our homes and to be able to read when and where we will. There was the time when it was unusual to find a Bible or even someone that could or even would dare to be found reading it. These men and women were indeed "strangers in the land of Canaan" so far as the freedom to read God's Word is concerned. Truly, we dwell in a land wherein they were once strangers. Then there were those who were "strangers in the land" because they could not conform to the state religion and felt that they ought to be able to worship God according to the dictates of their conscience, governed by the Word of God. They were strangers indeed. Many had to flee for their lives;

others died rather than bow down to the idolatrous practices of the day and the traditions of men. They were burnt at the stake, they were tortured on the rack to earn the freedom of worship that we enjoy today. There were those who fled the homeland to be strangers indeed on the far shores of the Americas. Today we enjoy the privileges for which they paid as strangers in a strange land. Let us dwell there and recognize our great heritage. We are free to hold the Word of God in our hands and we are free to worship as we desire to. But we could lose our rights and our privileges if we do not use them as we should. What we do not use, we lose. Our fathers paid the price to pioneer, let us not lightly esteem our inheritance, the inheritance they have left to us.

38. RUNNING AWAY

> *Genesis Chapter Thirty-eight, Verse One.*
> "And it came to pass at that time, that Judah
> went down from his brethren, and turned in
> to a certain Adullamite, whose name was
> Hirah."

"At that time." Could it be that Judah, with all
that had happened in the past concerning Joseph,
was seeking a way of escape from a guilty conscience
that bothered him? It can be that there comes a time
when men are tired of the ways of those with whom
they associate, their companions in the paths of sin
and deceit. Each man knows too much about the
other. And then there is always that in a man that
readily blames the other for what has happened, and
for present circumstances. Was Judah hoping that by
getting away from his brothers he could forget the
past, how that he, along with them, had almost
committed murder? None of us can escape the con-
sequences of our acts. We cannot hide our sins and
still prosper. They had sold Joseph as a slave and had
made their old father believe that Joseph had been
killed by a wild animal, and Jacob mourned him as
dead. What we sow we reap; that is the law of God.

Judah could turn from his brothers, but he could
not escape from God. No man outruns God. Judah
was to reap the heartaches that he had caused his
father. He "went down"—but his two sons, Er and

Onan, both die. Theirs was not a natural death, they were slain of the Lord.

The intention of the ten brothers was that Joseph should die and be forever forgotten. Men may forget, but God does not forget. Unless a man repents and puts the wrong right, he will surely reap what he has sown. Mercy can overrule justice. Mercy not only defers payment, but fully pardons the erring one and sets them free, with no condemnation. So stop running *away* from God, and run *to* Him, for He waits to forgive and forget.

> Oh! the love that drew salvation's plan,
> Oh! the grace that brought it down to man,
> Oh! the might gulf that God did span,
> At Calvary.

> Mercy there was great, and grace was free,
> Pardon there was multiplied to me,
> There my burdened soul found liberty,
> At Calvary.

39. THE FULFILLMENT OF DREAMS

Genesis Chapter Thirty-nine, Verse One.
"And Joseph was brought down to Egypt; and Potiphar, an officer of Pharaoh, captain of the guard, an Egyptian, bought him of the hands of the Ishmeelites, which had brought him down thither."

It was a long way from the Vale of Hebron to Egypt. Joseph could not understand what was happening to him at the time. What had begun as a day of seeking the welfare of his brethren passed into days of hot, wearisome travel down into Egypt as a slave, ready to be sold for the best price to whosoever would buy. At seventeen years of age many things are but mysteries. To this teenage youth there were a thousand questions to be answered: Why do I have to go through all this? If there is a God, why does He not do something for me now? We have sung many times in our services and particularly at a consecration service,

> I'll go where You want me to go, dear Lord,
>   Over mountain, or plain, or sea;
> I'll say what You want me to say, dear Lord,
>   I'll be what You want me to be.

The conjuror may wave a wand and bring a rabbit out of a hat, or pull yards of colored ribbon from his mouth; but there are some things that only God can work out, not by a wave of the hand, but through the paths He has chosen for us. It took four

87

thousand years to manifest His Son as the Redeemer and Savior. Although the promise had been given long before, there were many things to be filled in by Him. There are certain circumstances in your life and mine, and they are the only way through which God can fulfill His plan for us. If we are what we say we are, if we love the Lord as we say we love Him, then if He has to take us in certain paths that are unfamiliar, lonely, difficult, sorrowful—if this is the way to fulfill His will for us, then we ought to be willing.

It was said of Jesus, "Though he were a Son, yet he learned obedience by the things which he suffered. And being made perfect, he became the author of eternal salvation unto all them that obey him" (Heb. 5:8-9). To see into tomorrow is the privilege and the prerogative of God. To trust God for the tomorrows is the privilege of the believer.

> Trust Him when dark days assail thee,
>   Trust Him when thy faith is small,
> Trust Him when, to simply trust Him,
>   Is the hardest test of all.

40. WHERE ARE MY VISIONS?

Genesis Chapter Forty, Verse One.
"And it came to pass after these things, that the butler of the king of Egypt and his baker had offended their lord the king of Egypt."

A butler and a baker who had done some unknown deed offended their master, the king of Egypt. I am certain that down in Egypt the event had caused little stir, and possibly it was not even noticed, except in the servants quarters of the royal household. After all, a servant was only a servant subject to the whims and changes of the temperament of his master.

Something happens in your life, and mine, and at the moment it occurs we put little significance on it; but the small things fashion our lives and our future. If we really believe what God has said, we will be saved a lot of anxiety and care—knowing that God is working out His purpose, not only for us, but for others also. "And we know that all things work together for good to them that love God, to them who are the called according to his purpose" (Rom. 8:28). How often when we are in difficult situations we can see only how it affects *us*. None of the followers of Jesus could understand why He continually said He was going to die. They could only see a king and a conqueror. They thought only of an earthly kingdom of power, of

89

positions to be held and competed for. The ultimates of life are often veiled by the intermediates we have to pass through. Do we accept the Word of God only when it is for our immediate profit? So often we are too short-sighted, because we cannot see any farther than our own interests. "Looking unto Jesus, the author and finisher of our faith; who for the joy that was set before him endured the cross, despising the shame, and is set down at the right hand of the throne of God" (Heb. 12:2). It is not what is in time only that is final, it is that which shall be in the eternal. The eternal will be determined by that which we accept and pass through in this life. The ordinary events in your life and mine are the events that will change us for the future.

41. TIME WILL TELL

Genesis Chapter Forty-one, Verse One.
"And it came to pass at the end of two full years, that Pharaoh dreamed: and, behold, he stood by the river."

Everything in our lives has a time and a place. To the believer, to walk with God is to walk in the divine order. The sinner also, whether he believes it or not, is in the plan of God. For Pharaoh, the two years had come to a complete end. But it was not only for Pharaoh's sake that the dream was given at that exact time. He would hardly have believed it had he been told that a prisoner was involved in his dream and its fulfillment. Little did he know that the dream would drastically affect a man called Joseph who was in prison, and this man's family, headed by a man named Jacob. How far-reaching was that dream! It was to touch lives unthought of or unheard of in Egypt, as well as that of one man who was suffering from loss of memory of a good deed done to him years before. "Two full years." God is always on time and never before His time. We read concerning Jesus, "But when the fullness of the time was come, God sent forth his son" (Gal. 4:4). All things had to be ready for Jesus to come. Nothing happens to us by chance. If there is a delay in some program in our life, the delay is necessary for us, and possibly others are involved that we do not yet know about. Or, if suddenly we are confronted with the unexpected, then it is the day, the hour of our visitation. The one thing we must be is ready for anything.

> Ready for all Thy perfect will,
>   My acts of faith and love repeat,
> Till death thine endless mercies seal,
>   And make the sacrifice complete.

The Lord was never in the wrong place at the wrong time. He journeyed through Samaria just as the woman was at the well. Another journey took Him on the road where Bartimaeus was walking. Each time you will notice that He was at the right place at the right time. He died at the right moment, and rose again on the third day, as He said. Let us learn afresh that God has appointed times for all men and all things. Time must be fulfilled in our personal lives even as the two full years had to elapse in Pharaoh's life. "My times are in thy hands" (Ps. 31:15).

42. YOU DO SOMETHING ABOUT IT

Genesis Chapter Forty-Two, Verse One.
"Now when Jacob saw that there was corn in Egypt, Jacob said unto his sons, Why do ye look one upon another?"

It is a never-ending wonder to me to look on and to see the way one waits for the other to do something to meet a need. How true this is of many believers who want to do something for God if they can get someone else involved with them. Generally, it has been individuals who finally became totally involved who did something worthwhile for God. The sons of Jacob saw the need, they saw the stocks of grain dwindle with no replacement available. It is evident from the words of Jacob that his sons had been looking at each other, hoping the other would have the answer and would do something to bring about deliverance. The man at the pool of Bethesda in John 5 was looking at every man that came to the pool to help him get into the water that he might be healed. In the things of God it is often the case that everybody waits for another, and they themselves do nothing at all. Was it that Jacob saw others returning from Egypt with corn? Stirred by what he saw, he spoke. There were two things that made him speak. He saw a plentiful supply of corn to meet their need, and ten sons who made no effort to obtain the corn. He cried, "Why do ye look one to another?" Could it be true that the Lord is thinking the same of some of us His children? There is corn, there is meat, there is all that we could ever need for spirit, soul, and body in the redemption that Jesus has obtained for us. We half-heartedly look at each other and do not go in to possess our heritage. "He that spared not his own Son, but delivered him up for us all, how shall he not with him also freely give us all things?" (Rom. 8:32). Let us not stand looking at each other any longer. Let us not gaze upon the corn, but let us go in and possess the purchased possession. Let us not be mutual admirers, but mutual participators.

43. ADVERSITY A BLESSING

Genesis Chapter Forty-three, Verse One.
"And the famine was sore in the land."

A bare, cold, factual statement that cries out for attention—how often in life it is the casual statement that goes unheeded, often unheard. So many times the situation has to become desperate before any notice is taken at all. At the beginning of the mentioned famine there were only a few people affected, but as it continued, more and more became involved, and only then was the severity of the situation realized. Everyone feels the sharp demands that it is making upon their lives.

There are situations in life that arise and some prefer to ignore, but as the condition persists and worsens, we are compelled to take notice. We are living in days when little by little many of our Christian privileges are being quietly whittled away. How many of us have really thought of the change that came about when the government changed the name of "Whitsuntide Holiday" to the "Spring Holiday"? To many it matters not what the holiday is called, but in reality this change begins to take that day away from the church calendar. Who knows when and where the next change will come? Did Daniel forsee these days? "And he shall speak great words against the most High, and think to change times and laws" (Dan. 7:24-25). How much more do we have to lose before we notice the famine that is among us? The desire for the Word of God is less and less these days. Many other things take its place. What we do not cherish, we will soon see perish. God has said, "Behold the days come, saith the Lord God, that I will send a famine in the land, not a famine of bread, nor a thirst for water, but of hearing the words of the Lord" (Amos 8:11).

As it was, all the people touched by the famine had to go to Joseph to have their needs supplied. Let us who are of the household of faith go to Jesus, who this day will satisfy our hungry hearts. "Arise and shine; for thy light is come, and the glory of the Lord is risen upon thee" (Isa. 60:1).

44. EMPTY STOMACHS— FULL SACKS

Genesis Chapter Forty-Four, Verse One.
"And he commanded the steward of his house, saying, Fill the men's sacks with food, as much as they can carry, and put every man's money in his sack's mouth."

The liberality of Joseph to his brethren is a wonderful example of forgiveness. These same brethren, in their envy and jealousy, had sold Joseph as a slave for twenty pieces of silver. Now, about fifteen years later, he sits upon the throne of Egypt, ruling for Pharaoh. When his brothers bowed down before him, his dreams were being fulfilled. But no recriminations are heard. The past was forgiven: Fill their sacks, as much as they can carry, put in their money again!

Oh! The grace of God to us today. We rebelled against God, but He comes to us and says to Jesus, Fill their sacks, as much as they can carry, without charge. "Ho, everyone that thirsteth, come ye, buy and eat, yea, come, buy wine and milk without money and without price" (Isa. 55:1). "Blessed be the Lord, who daily loadeth us with benefits, even the God of our salvation" (Ps. 68:19). The more we come to Him, in entire dependence upon Him, the more He loves to give to us. Each time we come He will give us as much as we can carry away. I heard only yesterday of a girl who worked in a launderette. Each day the dimes (used in the machines) were emptied into a large container. The girl was a Christian and needed money to go to a Christian camp. Her employer said that she could practice for one week, seeing how many dimes she could pick up in one handful without cupping her hand upwards, and that she could have all she could hold for the camp. On the day appointed, her employer said, "Now, are you ready? Whatever you pick up today is yours." It would be sufficient to say that she went to the camp meeting.

"As much as they can carry away." There are many restaurants that offer all that you can eat for a nominal price. A sign in one such restaurant says, "Take all that you can eat, eat all that you take." In this great salvation, we can, in Christ, have as much of the life of Christ that we can carry. Lord, enlarge our capacity for more of Yourself.

Filled with God, yes, filled with God,
　　Pardoned and cleansed and filled with God,
Filled with God, yes, filled with God,
　　Emptied of self and filled with God.

45. THE LOVE OF JESUS

Genesis Chapter Forty-five, Verse One.
"Then Joseph could not refrain himself
before all them that stood by him; and he
cried, Cause every man to go out from me.
And there stood no man with him, while
Joseph made himself known unto his
brethren."

There is a limit to the emotions the heart and
mind can endure. The time comes in the lives of
men, even strong men, when they weep. God
created us with emotions. To "love" without emotion is to not love at all. We may restrain ourselves,
hide our feelings, but if we continue to do so, we
hurt ourselves. The life in the Spirit is the life that
produces fruit, the fruit of the Spirit. This fruit
grows as the expression of what is within and what
is nurtured. When a believer is conscious of being
full of Christ, he is full of love. What an impossibility, to be full of love and to refrain one's self from
loving! To have the knowledge of sins forgiven; to
know that you have eternal life, and to understand
that God is your Father and heaven is your home
because Christ is your Savior is surely enough to
fill you with joy. And with such knowledge and
such joy, how can we refrain our hearts from worship and praise any longer, as Jesus, our heavenly
Joseph, makes Himself known to us? "Whom having not seen, ye love; in whom, though now ye see
him not, yet believing, ye rejoice with joy un-

speakable and full of glory" (1 Peter 1:8). Jesus said, "I will see you again, and your heart shall rejoice, and your joy no man taketh from you" (John 16:22). Let us not refrain ourselves any longer from the praise that is due to His name, lest we be rebuked by the stones: "And when he was come nigh, even now at the descent of the mount of Olives, the whole multitude of the disciples began to rejoice and praise God with a loud voice for all the mighty works that they had seen . . . and some of the Pharisees . . . said unto him, Master, rebuke thy disciples. And he answered and said unto them, I tell you that, if these should hold their peace, the stones would immediately cry out" (Luke 19:37-40). We can no longer refrain ourselves, we must cry out. Hallelujah! to the Lamb of God.

46. THE LAST PILGRIMAGE

Genesis Chapter Forty-six, Verse One.
"And Israel took his journey with all that he had, and came to Beersheba, and offered sacrifices unto the God of his father Isaac."

This was to be the last journey that Israel was to take. He was going to see his son—the son that to him had been dead for all these years, but now was reported to be alive. What were the evidences of his being alive? What was it that made Israel believe this? The evidences of Joseph being alive were the gifts that he had sent: the wagons, and the provisions all around him, sent by his son to bring him on the way to where he was. We, too, are taking our journey at the moment with all that we have, whether it be much or little. We are on our way to see the Son. They did say that He was dead, yes, He *had* died, but He is alive forevermore.

As Israel came on his journey, he came to Beersheba. This was the place where Abraham met the Everlasting God who had assured him of a safe pilgrimage. So here, too, God meets Israel and, strange enough, calls him by his old name *Jacob*. "Jacob! Jacob!" Why did He revert to the name *Jacob*? Because Jacob is fearful of the journey into a strange land at this time of life. The Everlasting God of Beer-sheba, assures him "Fear not to go down into Egypt, for I will make of thee a great nation" (Gen. 46:3).

Many fear the unknown. But we have His promise, "I will never leave thee nor forsake thee" (Heb. 13:5). Many who were ahead of us have already arrived, and each day the line is moving up. We are on our journey to see the Son. As we go we take everything along with us, but at the last stage of the journey we shall leave everything behind. When we see Him, the Son, we shall be like Him, and nothing on earth will be of any value. We shall have arrived and be reunited with our Heavenly Joseph. "Wherefore seeing we also are compassed about with so great a cloud of witnesses, let us lay aside every weight, and the sin which doth so easily beset us, and let us run with patience the race that is set before us. Looking unto Jesus . . ." (Heb. 12:1-2).

47. IDENTIFICATION— MY FATHER

> *Genesis Chapter Forty-seven, Verse One.*
> "Then Joseph came and told Pharaoh, and
> said, My father and my brethren, and their
> flocks, and their herds, and all that they
> have, are come out of the land of Canaan;
> and behold, they are in the land of
> Goshen."

This personal announcement of Joseph to
Pharaoh of the arrival of his father and brothers
with their flocks and herds was a wonderful dis-
play of identification with his own people. Joseph
was reckoned as an Egyptian, and for an Egyptian
to fellowship with these shepherds and herdsmen
was an abomination to the Egyptians, But he
boldly says, "My father! . . . my brethren!" The
Egyptian dynasty of that day was made up of
highly educated and intellectual people. The
brothers of Joseph were shepherds, just ordinary,
simple, country men, unsophisticated, and used
only to the life of the country. This probably
showed in their dress and manners.

We can praise the Lord for His grace and His
great salvation that sent Jesus to redeem us—those
of us who were of low degree, and also those of
high degree. He made us all to be one in Himself.
"But we see Jesus, who was made a little lower than
the angels for the suffering of death, crowned with
glory and honor; that he by the grace of God should

taste death for every man. . . . For both he that sanctifieth and they who are sanctified are all one: for which cause he is not ashamed to call them brethren" (Heb. 2:9-11). Israel and his sons, and all they were, were accepted because of Joseph. Pharaoh bestowed upon them all that Joseph desired them to have. All that Pharaoh did for them, was done because of the honor and glory of Joseph. God has given to us all things that pertain unto life, because of Jesus. Jesus was identified with the throne of God, and He then identified Himself with us, and we now in turn are identified with Him in His glory. He can say of us, My brethren! "But God, who is rich in mercy, for his great love wherewith he loved us, even when we were dead in sins, hath quickened us together with Christ (by grace ye are saved); and hath raised us up together, and made us sit together in heavenly places in Christ Jesus" (Eph. 2:4-6).

48. THE HANDS OF BENEDICTION

Genesis Chapter Forty-eight, Verse One.
"And it came to pass after these things,
that one told Joseph, Behold, thy father is
sick: and he took with him his two sons,
Manasseh and Ephraim."

In this visit to his sick and dying father, Joseph
was thinking of a blessing for his two sons. There
are many times when one visits the sick with the
intention of comforting them and finding oneself
comforted instead. We often go to give to the sufferer, and it is the sufferer who gives to us, and *we*
leave with a blessing. Joseph leaves his place and
hurries over to his aging father. If the father might
only put his hands upon Manasseh and Ephraim.

There is a ministry of impartation from the Lord
through men of God. I can never forget the experience of the hands of Smith Wigglesworth being
laid on my head, and the unction of that Spirit-
filled life touching mine. There was another occa-
sion when, after much prayer and fasting, I asked
George Jeffries to lay his hands upon me that I
might be used in the ministry of the gifts of the
Spirit. I knew that the gifts are only given "as He
wills," but there *is* something in the heavenly impartation of the laying on of hands of the holy
anointed elder brethren. It is not a thing to be
lightly esteemed. The apostle Paul reminds
Timothy, "Wherefore I put thee in remembrance

that thou stir up the gift of God, which is in thee by the putting on of my hands" (2 Tim. 1:6). Interpret this as you will, it still remains.

Manasseh and Ephraim had known nothing of the laying on of the patriarchal hands of blessing, they being born in Egypt and raised in Egypt. But Joseph wanted them to know the blessing of the God of Abraham, of Isaac, and of Jacob from the lips of his father, Israel, and imparted through the laying on of the old man's hands. Let us not miss any opportunity that presents it self for blessing from these elder brethren among us who have been greatly used of God in the ministry of the Holy Spirit.

49. SONS OF GOD HAVE A FUTURE

Genesis Chapter Forty-nine, Verse One.
"And Jacob called unto his sons, and said,
Gather yourselves together, that I may tell
you that which shall befall you in the last
days."

Jacob had arrived at the end of his earthly
journey. It had been an eventful journey, with its
share of hazards and blessings. There had been the
sunshine and the rain, the storm and the calm
—and such is life. Without these experiences life
would be nothing, but the great thing is to come
out a victor at the end. It is with dignity and calm
that this patriarch calls his sons together as he is
about to make a presentation to them, not of gifts,
but of the foresight of the future for their lives. In
these final moments of his life, the father shows
himself the head of the family, not only as father,
but as a prophet, for he said, "That I may tell you
what may befall you in the last days." In the moments of death there can be no room for pretense or
hypocrisy. The curtain is drawn aside on reality.
Nothing is forgotten, and with precise
forethought, Jacob speaks to each of his sons. He
tells them what they have been, and what they are,
and then he speaks of what shall be for each of
them. There is here a Jacob, not with a beclouded
mind, but a clear-thinking man about to take a
journey of no return giving instructions to those he

is leaving behind. He tells them what to do and how to do it.

There is a place where we each can live, so that when we come to the moment of going over to the other side, it is not the unknown for us, for we have been enjoying our heaven all along the way. We can speak to those around us and leave them a heritage, not so much the silver and gold, but of that which shall be revealed to us of their lives for the future, if they will but obey. To order our lives in the will of God is to know His will to the end and to be able to bless our sons and daughters with the knowledge that the best is yet to be.

50. ULTIMATE DEVOTION —WORSHIP

Genesis Chapter Fifty, Verse One.
"And Joseph fell upon his father's face, and wept upon him, and kissed him."

Here is devotion from one who has loved deeply, and from one who has known what it was to have a period in his life of twenty years to have no father to counsel and guide him, from the age of seventeen, at a time when he needed him the most. There would be times when he wondered whether he was alive, and whether those dreams that he had dreamed were but the fancies of the night. Then to discover that his father was alive, and to see that the dreams were from God and were now being fulfilled! Having no bitterness against his brothers, he becomes a brother and a son, indeed. When Jacob died and Joseph wept over his father's dead body, he had no regrets. He had done everything in his power according to his station in life to bless him, and not only him, but all his father's house. There is no false sorrow here, no circumstantial emotion, no weeping of remorse for a memory of that which could have been done by him and was not. No! Here were tears of true sorrow. So often when loved ones have passed on, there have been the flowers of respect, and sometimes tears. In many cases it would have been much better had the flowers of respect been given while the loved one was alive. The world is full of neglected mothers and fathers. Many will receive more attention when they are dead than they received when they were alive. We know that there are the exceptional cases of none-too-good parents, but on the whole, let us give to our parents the respect and honor they deserve *while they live.* Joseph more than repaid his father for the seventeen years of care, love, and devotion that he had given to him. So, when we see our own pass on, let it be that we have no regrets, even though we may sorrow at their going, though not sorrowing as others who have no hope. While they live, let us do what we can according to our station in life. When they have died, we can do no more, but live for the glorious day of reuniting with them and with Him.

This book may also be secured from the author:

William Hartley
P.O. Box 8036
Prairie Village, Kansas 66208 U.S.A.